IN THE ARMS OF THE FATHER

POEMS

FLAVIA COSMA

Translated from the Romanian by Flavia Cosma
with Charles Siedlecki

ČERVENÁ BARVA PRESS
SOMERVILLE, MASSACHUSETTS

Červená Barva Press
P.O. Box 440357
W. Somerville, MA 02144-3222

www.cervenabarvapress.com
Bookstore: www.thelostbookshelf.com

Cover photo: Courtesy Wikimedia Commons

Cover Design: William J. Kelle
Production: Steve Asmussen

ISBN: 978-1-950063-05-5

Library of Congress Control Number: 2020947481

CONTENTS

IN THE ARMS OF THE FATHER

POEMS

Translated by Flavia Cosma with Charles Siedlecki

Third Prize 2007 Dryden Translation Competition—
British Comparative Literature Association/British Centre
for Literary Translation

Introduction to the Poet(ry)

Flavia Cosma's verse bids us enter a maze,
Boasting a guillotine at every turn and exit.
Her ink is shiny, but squirts out like venom.
Her pen is—correctly—as honed as a spear.

She realizes our world fields gilded coffins,
And Christians appear worse than sinners.
We shudder with disgust at *Death*; we say
It's disgusting. But our lives aren't tasteful.

Cosma scribes one steady stricture—a line:
Experience is *Innocence* put under *Torture*.
Thus, Plath is Dickinson freed from Gitmo,
And *Passions* run as manic as *Temptations*.

Cosma's lines shadow the joys of fairy-tales,
But her "Mother Goose" just masks Medusa.
We hear Xmas carols sung as sobbing dirges;
Infants go into ovens; manna flurries as ash.

Diligently moral, Cosma strives to find God,
Not in icons, but in fire that incinerates jails;
Or, not in hymns, but in the screams of nuns.
Flavia Cosma views The Garden after The Fall.

George Elliott Clarke
Poet Laureate of Toronto (2012-15)

HE, WHO IS CONSUMED BY FIRE,
WILL NEVER ROT.

Solitude

I could have copied
The thousands of sentences,
Wisely conceived,
Written or uttered
Throughout history.

I could nourish myself
On the sap of million of flowers
Carefully painted or sculpted
In the Gardens of Eden.

But I want to inscribe
On the blank page granted me,
Thoughts untouched by stellar dust,
Whispers dreamed only by myself,
Distinct, important days,
Mornings solely mine, on the calendar.

I want to be alone
In the blue shade of the stone;
Under ever-traveling skies
With my bare soles, to caress
The heads of saints, sleeping in prayer,
Who, sometimes,
Through earthen air,
Will breathe strength,
A sweet and gentle breeze,
From their minds
Into my savage blood.

In the Arms of The Father

In the arms of The Father
We soar in the morning.
The sun, a silver salver,
Holds us tight in its great embrace.

Severe and shining,
How cold today are the arms of The Father!

Suave birds' necks, napes of angels,
Lie in wait, twisting, on the river's banks,
Hallowed, modest branches
Reflect themselves in waters.

We promise each other eternal love;
Silky words float softly through the air,
We give each other butterflies made of ice;
We bestow forgiveness on our fiercest enemies;
Like a dome, the non-pain, an absolute void,
Weighs heavily on old, white spines.
It rains with large, rust-colored drops;
The flood is catching up with us,
Seizes us,
Carries us into the arms of The Father,
Into stillness.

WHEN UNAWARE STILL...

Attentively, the snakes, avoided me with care,
When of snakes I didn't know yet,
Swarms of wasps protected me
When of venom I was unaware;
Friendly porcupines enwrapped me
In the soft and deep green
Of the walnut's grass, in the garden.

I didn't know a thing about any of these.

Nothing could stand up against me,
No wall was too high for me to climb,
No burden too heavy,
No humiliation
To hurt me that much.

I knew nothing of any of these.

My house teems today with winged insects;
My mattress is alive with silvery snakes;
Poisons lie in wait on the spear tips of leaves.

The withered grass lures me with the taste of death;
The tiger licks its muzzle, smiles,
Spent years uncoil before my eyes,
In dark and long lines,
One after the other.

REVERIE

The Sun,
A fleshy flower,
Drops with a sound
Beyond the house.

Sun of a flower,
Sun-butterfly,
Ruffled silk,
Shining rainbow.

Where does the tunnel,
Through the heart of an apple lead to?

The wind sings wistfully
Night after night,
At the window.

Your frowning Eyes glare at me
From paper faces;
Who saddened You Lord
With all these low mists?

Smooth your forehead, Father,
Erase the red mark between your furrowed eyebrows;
There is order in the Universe,
There is quiet;
The branch is warm, full of flowers;
The night's song can also become
A sweet, gentle whisper.

The Infant sits like a ray,
In the Holy Virgin's lap;
Two little stars steal out
From the Christmas tree,
Hanging fragile
In a gilded frame.

At the white sea shore,
On the steps of Your temple,
The Child is playing,
Eyes us cheerfully;
He doesn't know yet
The ways of this world.

Sacred Places

There are places I am still passing,
Which surround me once more with their wan happiness.

Here, under the neon lights, by the entrance,
I was startled by his timid kiss,
Like a soft evening breeze,
Like a wavering
Question mark.

Going back on the stony bridge
I stumble on the valley bathed in moonlight;
Around us, a soft, little song,
The mysterious whisper of the summer's night.
We were two milky fires,
Phosphorescent, ardent,
With the haste of the first and the last sparkle.

I see again the joyful and young shadows,
Harmony's fragrance spreads through the ether,
The suave embrace flows impetuously
From veins unseen
Into my thirsty body,
More careworn by the world's passions,
More parched.

THE SALTED TASTE OF DEATH

Apocalypse Now (Christmas 2004)

All the ocean's waves converged into one,
Stately spreading over the quick sands,
Over the blue desert, over the sigh.
The Divine Hand forcefully struck
The earth and its bearings,
The abundance.
"This is just to remind you."
Said He,
"Or just Destiny."
In His great haste
He crumbled away walls, parapets,
With a fiery rumble, like matches.
Forgotten in the sun, the human shells,
Lay in heaps, babbling, slowly rotting.
Through heavy, ephemeral air,
Yellow smoke rises to heavens,
Like a final whisper asking for forgiveness.

ON THREADS OF CIGARETTE SMOKE

On threads of cigarette smoke
The whimper of the wind rises in the sky,
Like the prolonged wailing
Of a wild cub.

Mysterious, the soft-stepping night
Spreads out at the foot of the river.
In February's brittle air
Thought struggles to find again
Its path, lost through time.

The discarded apple rolls between us
Like shiny water gulped down by rocks.
You don't see me -
But you're still eying me;
I am still talking
Not knowing what I'm saying;
The words—colored, glassy marbles—
Slide slowly on the wooden table;
Dry frost takes us
By our bare shoulders.

In this place our ancestors dug
Sepulchers in stone.
Broken mouths of pitchers
Cover the ground;
The river, a gray animal,
Breathes heavily.

Untouched by the wings of time,
The suspicion and the lying in wait
Come to life in your hands,
Distrustfully spread on the table,
Like some white, hostile daggers.

I know it's the hour
To drag the dream out of its cage,
To chase the illusion of endless love.
Long lasting bridges,
Continuity,
Painstakingly melted into futility,
Sink into furrows of mud.

From a high bank I hurl harsh words;
Through clenched teeth
I spit them out fast and rejoice;
I hear them splashing, noisily plunging.
The waters roar, the fir tree sighs,
Mermaids of silt and ice urge us,
—Our fists gripping marbles and knives,—
To jump into the barbarous hollow,
To be far away
From ourselves.

THE OLDEST OF THE OLD

The oldest of old people
And newly born infants
Share equally
The same vague look.

Where do they walk
A path together?
And where do they meet?
In which all-glorious place?

The figure, the colors, the voice,
Sift one after another later on,
According to how the winds blow in Eternity,
According to how the claws of time scrape.

God has promised
And lets you chose
Both shortcomings and gifts
From the ancestors' garden:
The fretting, the vanity,
The arrogance, the cowardice,
The bravery, the joy.

In your small chest you gather everything
And grow up with it, straighter or more twisted,
Only to give it back
When the hour comes
On the high, clay threshold.

Why then the dying
Disgusts us so deeply?

Melt your heart, Stone,
And you Sky take pity
In the presence of this very short journey;
You who are almost immortal
Like the Gods,
Hoard all the world's seeds
In vast granaries
And devotedly save
The sacred wine of living
In holy ewers.

Study well your words, Soul,
Because all things scatter, blown in the wind;
Raise for yourself, from words, a lasting statue,
Build wisely a solid foundation,
A dam against dissonant, frantic tremors,
That the turbid waters
May not raze your creation
From the earth's face.

TRINITY

Three green peas on the plate,
Three tears lingering on the face,
Three grapes,
Three spoons set at the table,
The Holy Trinity, with soft fingers,
Descends on a ray
Into the house.

Both The Father and The Son and even
The Holy Ghost
Thoroughly examine us.
They ponder how, from straying ways
To turn us back,
Pushing us with an old hand
Onto the well-known chaste path.

The sky whitens from so much strain.
The Father's wrath is showing wholly,
The mind still fights,
The heart—the sacred fires' dwelling—
Ailing, throbs.

Father, if it wasn't You who created love,
The sweet poison trickling into our knees,
The wavering, yet bold step,
The eyelid's quiver in spent quietness,
Who, then, burns
Our days, our nights?

What illness, what passions are shaking
Our doors from under their arms,
And blinding our windows with tears?
What temptation keeps
The soul eager and awake?

At Dawn

When the day interweaves with the night,
And silences disappear into soft cooing,
The winter with its pointed ears
Feels its way through autumn back to us.

Good spirits in low bands,
Surround us on the wooden stair,
Peace takes us by the hand, resurrects us,
Wants us to be awake when wellness seizes us,
To our bones' cores,
Beautifully.

On young thresholds carols bud,
Pine trees with heavy skirts
Shake off their thoughts;
As in every year we renew our being,
Our scrap of light,
Pure, turns back to us.

Deep voiced bells solemnly herald;
Sleep, a tangled ball,
Slips from eyelids.
Yellowed flowers shining freeze,
Astonished, day slowly arises
From a stony dream.

ANNIVERSARY

You have died, Ana Teoran,
Beautiful girl,
With time, your children have drowned in their turn,
Only I am left to reminisce about you;
Beautiful girl,
I don't remember you too well either.

Your sparkling teeth,
Your laugh,
The child crying;
Oh! Beautiful girl,
Grief breaks my heart.

BETWEEN TWO OF YOUR WORDS...

Between two of your words
I stop and I weep;
I hear my voice trying to keep back
My unstable balance, the equilibrium;
I hear the space, the void,
Rustling between us,
The cunning claw of the night
Near the house,
Scraping.

I rise on tiptoes
And I still think I'm flying;
At the same time,
Nothingness stretches up on tiptoes
Beside me;
Sonorous ripples
Flounder
In the ocean's depths.

How prolonged is
This imaginary journey!
Infinity is casting off its babies
One after another
On the ashen path.

Midnight Thoughts

At midnight, the flowers
Rise to their feet,
The distance, an unwritten book,
Waits beneath the window,
                    hand in hand with the moon.
Hungry wasps throng
On finger tips, sweet petals,
The wind whispers, softly breezes.
Imaginary, fast earwigs,
Cross our thoughts
In orderly rows.

Their long necks sticking out of the sand,
Hydras strive to swallow
Skeletons of stone.
The stab in the ribs becomes a white cat.
The straight line,
A sign of perfection,
Lags behind, waiting.

Mists and smoke piously emerge from chasms,
Like a giant, collective soul,
The rock melts into silky soils,
The sand, the grass, the dogs,
Take the shape of a wave,
Wave twisting over wave,
Climbing freely
Toward the sky.

GRANDMOTHER

With heavy perfumes
Of lilac in bloom,
On airy threads, once more,
You're entering the room.
Grandmother, sweet Grandmother,
Clusters of lilacs sway on their branches,
The summer, freshly born,
Draws you back from memory.

A little girl again, I find myself beside you,
Bathing into your fair and ancient image,
In a mysterious instant I open big cupboards
And bury my face in folds of heavy silks.

Musty fear springs up from drawers;
I hate time, impetuous and too brief;
I wasn't your child,
Neither were you my mother,
The fruits of past summers
Do not cohabit
With flowers yet unborn, still undreamt of.

Lightly, the lamp's flame resurrects you,
With your quarrels and your words,
With great worries, with patched-up days,
With your tired, tender hands.

I see in the mirror how the years keep flowing
On faces of stone and clay;
It's already my turn to descend,
To be like you were,
Courageous.
To hurl the rock-like pain
Of great losses—
A clawed cat—
Into younger laps,
Into the times to come.

SPIDER-LIKE STAR

A spider-like star dancing before me
Guides my steps through a maze.
It sprigs up contentedly on threads of the sky,
Above the sea's dried up bed,
In a place where once majestic ships
Heavy with precious stones and silver coins,
Rocked their stately hulls
On the waves;
The same place where
Dark, boiling mud
Reigns undisturbed today.

Vapid Love

Melancholy, like a cupola,
Descends with winter in the afternoon.

Under blanched fingers of branches,
Light, weakened, starts;
The sound flows, sweet venom,
Longing bites our beings in full,
Anxieties keep our hearts awake.

Vapid love,
Pure seduction of death,
A wax leaf burns
Glued to the soft trunk of a candle;
Its veins, suave fans,
Cower, changing into ashes;
The flame gulps greedily
The seen and the unseen alike,
The blue snow and the mists.
A bird enwraps me like a ghost.

All knowing,
The glassy eye of the moon
Covers the ice.

THE OMENS

Green arabesques
Frame the window.
The frail lemon tree is invaded by flowers,
Each line is an alarm signal,
Fleshy, wide leaves
Are full of future worries;
Outside, it snows frosty grains,
The wind sweeps away masses of snow,
Sadness, in its yellow skirts,
Writhes.

Everywhere, only forewarning signs,
Only harsh fingers pointing at the void,
Under a heap of glossy words
Temptations transform themselves into great dangers,
Hollow screams fill up eardrums,
Fistfuls of air disappear roaring
Under lowly fogs,
The heart's rhythms change into
                    the chattering of teeth,
The sea swallows in its blue waves
Obedient, as yet unborn dreams.

Smoky offerings circle round the vault,
We hear nothing; we feel nothing;
Nothing was left that is ours,
Willing to decipher
Everybody's desire,
We rush ourselves,
We suffer.

I Knew These Verses ...

I knew these verses before,
    but today,
They spring up in a different way,
     —more loved—
The hand is steadier,
The voice softer,
The cloud breathes in sapphire
     from a song.

From the great abyss
Friends entice me
With playful rhymes;
A ball of ice stumbles on the road,
The fog lifts a corner of its kerchief,
Now and then it snows petals of thoughts,
The old willow leafs out in its dream,
Anemic colors scatter into ether,
The air is velvety, scented,
From its own sleep,
Sleep
Awakens.

FINDING YOU AGAIN

You,
As much unknown to me,
As falling raindrops on blue flowers,
You,
As necessary to me,
As the pure air, seeping into my lungs,
You,
As much precious to me,
As golden light gliding through stained glass panes
Over hands clasped together in prayer,
Invoking peace, forgiveness,
And above all
Love,

You,
One day you will cross the sea and all the forests,
Weary, you'll stop in front of my gates,
And I'll welcome you, seized by a holy shiver,
My eyes filled with tears, and my soul a nest
To belated, mellow loves.
Oh, beggar...

THE WHITE MINUTE

Without warning,
A white minute, with its pale, righteous face,
Chases me out of sleep.
What wrong did I do,
What injustice,
Hunts me fiercely
Like a watchful, soaring eagle?

Could I have somewhat changed the drenched dream?
Or the blue snow, creaking under foot?
The water weeds gnawing at the horn of the moon?
Or the peacocks, so full of themselves?

Fear—a soft cat—
Oozes into the room.
Many spells and temptations
Mount the threshold.
A streak of light wraps itself in a cloud.
Nor is my sleep calm,
But when I am awake,
All burdens weigh on me,
My saps hurt.

Don't Throw Gold Coins at Me...

Don't throw gold coins in heaps at me
So forcefully, with hands full, through the window.
You overwhelm me with so many splendors.

I feel your beautiful and golden train
Tenderly quivering by the window pane
And your voice, modulated, deep,
Whispering daring tales in my ear
 During long, silky midnights.

Don't linger with your white, soft palms,
Waiting to cool my longing in the morning,
The happiness, too full, too round,
Struggles to make its way through memories
From the time of our first encounters,
When our steps were small, childlike,
And full of loving wandered
The vast world over.

Awkward Sleep

When heavy sleep seizes me,
My last thought
Drags me back to you,
To your constant worry of squandering me
Through unseeing fingers, in space.

When I think of you
Sleeps seizes me heavily,
A blessed cure,
A balm and a spell.

In somnambular throes
I climb and descend
Uneven, slippery stairs,
As senseless words stand guard.

Nothingness, both yellow and bitter,
Surrounds me
Like a humid, soiled mantle,
Slipping cold from my shoulders
With every whimper heard outside,
With every footstep on the pavement.

From one obscurity into another;
I grope and I jump.
I long hopelessly for a bear, for a hero,
I want to weigh the lance in both hands,
To slit open the fog, as I would a beast's belly,
To soar freely into a hoary light,
To fly without wings.

SMALL BIRD

Small bird, little girl bird,
It's so hard for me to nurse you,
I'm so loathe to touch you.

You knocked yourself hard against the window pane;
How were you to know where the sky ended?
Your wings stretched out on a gray slab,
Your half closed, glassy eyes,
I waited for you
To pass over, in death.

But the thin thread wouldn't break,
Your heart, a fist, continued throbbing.
Your mother flying by, scolded you, called for you.
The sly cat lay in wait on the fence.

Clumsily you stood on one foot,
The other hurt you so.
I picked you up; I enclosed you in a card box;
Later I found you standing on top,
Your head lost in thoughts,
Perched now on one shoulder,
Then on the other.

For an instant I didn't watch you;
I turned back; you were gone,
The wind had lifted you into a fairy tale.

The sky teems with birds, and with mothers;
I remain here holding still in my hands
Your golden feather, a slight testimony
Of your passing through,
Little fragile bird,
Small terrestrial joy.

ANCESTORS

I burned the elders
In their small, votive lamps,
—White and blue gold—
In the room's corners.

Cleansed lights
Hang on fir-tree branches,
To a damp Christmas
Ford and long lasting
Footbridge.

Eagerly,
I stretch out my hand
Over deep oceans.
I rummage in haste
The downy snows;
I rediscover toys, diminutive (miniature) houses,
How large they seemed once!
When roving carefree
I would lose myself
In rooms with low ceilings.

Dear friends smile at me
From enchanting post-cards.
We meet in the morning with colorful greetings.
We start again our lively reels,
We leap cheerfully many thresholds backwards.
Heavy with fruit orchards,
Endless plains in bloom,
And ancient rays, woven into mysteries,
Entice us from beyond.

THE POISON

The serpent bit me
Hundreds of times,
While Mars, red and glowing,
Jumped on the vault
Now under the moon,
Then over a cloud.

A green flying insect
Stands guard over my sleep;
In flight, a hurried wing touches me;
The serpent's venom permeates my veins;
My hand spills a poisonous, purple wave
Onto blank sheets of paper;
Bitterness rises, a harsh lump in my throat;
The sun burns and withers away,
The sea, a wild beast,
Throws itself about, howls.

The unquiet red mushroom,
Boasting,
Beautiful,
Keeps growing at my feet.

From my weepy sleep
A flying insect awakens me;
Perching on my ailing hand
A transparent shadow.

I know I'll crush its fragile life
When I come to remove it;
Nevertheless, the green, good omen,
Will follow me the whole day
With its frail translucent wing.

So Many Clocks in the House

There are so many clocks in the house.
Some work fast, hastening the hour,
Others linger, further and further backward.
My watch, though, marks the time sharply,
The exact hour, the just hour,
The wise hour.

Clocks set free, clocks scattered,
In humid corners, monotonously ticking;
Cardboard clocks, gilded clocks,
Time pours forth from objects, on a string.

The frenzied race holds us to the spot.
Withered hands tremble on leaves of paper,
Deepened, the brow fold carefully measures
The barren hour, the desiccated instants,
The days - flags fluttering at gates -
The kid jumping over rocks,
The bitter salt in locks.

We breathe onto our palms a foolish joy,
Thinking we are soaring into freedom;
The hands of the clock lie greedily in wait,
And cut short our flight,
Our bird's flight.

Deceptive Seas

Like you, I have seen
The baby face of seduction;
I have rocked, like you,
On these deceptive seas.
Like many others, I myself have gathered,
Salted grains of sweat
From ardent, fiery lips.

Eyelashes of sand
Bow softly over
The moon's stony eye.
Indifferent,
The sun sets.
Twilight's spirit glides into us,
At the gate, a Lebanese cedar
Rustles gently.

Much as we would like to,
We cannot succeed
In fooling fate.
A day passes, then two nights,
Eternity;
Overwhelmed by helplessness we fall asleep;
Silvery mantles sway slowly on the crests;
Life goes, an ephemeral tale.

And I, who have thought
That we
Loved each other.

The Ashen Instant

"Why are you crying, Mother?"
"Because I have no child."
"And why do you cry, little one?"
"I have no one either,
I am an orphan too."

In an ashen instant
Worries surround us with large, unfurling wings,
Quietly, snakes fall asleep
Near the roots of the grass;
Lofty trees comb their manes,
Continue growing;
White hot, future summers,
Hover about
In our evening thoughts.

Merciful, the earth
Bears with us another year.

Sweating peasants diligently plough the sod,
Deep and black ridges appear in their wake,
In their open palms, feeling the seeds.
Fleeting miracles
Perpetuate life.

Neither the shy angels sent to protect us,
Nor the pale deceased whispering in prayer,
Can't guess our sorrow, our helplessness;
Unable to grasp the advice,
We don't follow it
Even if we listen.

FOLLOWING IN THE POET'S FOOTSTEPS

Following in the Poet's footsteps
We strip grounded ships of their jewels
On blinded, desolate shores.

Our eyes burn in the smoky sun,
Rays dance on the flimsy vault,
Whispered words glide through air;
The hesitant steps of the Poet
Approach in the distance.

On invisible threads
A spider descends into the room.
Harsh signs descending into the room
                          alongside it.
The wound awakens in the chest
Beneath barbarously imprinted boots,
Eyelids flutter,
The heart starts.

We know now
          what we searched for,
                    never found
Under cypresses old as the world:
Women with pealing voices and soft waving hands,
Embroidering with gold threads in mornings
A sacred, rare word,
The returning steps of the Poet,
On silks filled with grace.

In inexpressible wonder we watch
The precious footprints that come and go,
Like a tide on a smooth sea,
Like a baby of a cloud, on a clear sky.

Each step, every gesture,
Hides in its core the accident, the upset,
The fragile stumble,
The End,
The healing footsteps of the Poet.

Every step forward
Follows naturally after another,
Repeating it humbly,
Living it reverently,
Meeting it
In saintly awe.

The Most Terrible Frost

Everything is crumbling under a terrible frost.
Some of us still believe and still hope.
Leaves, reddened by martyrs' blood,
Drop heavily to the ground
                   — poor inebriated girls—
Flocks of crows are blooming as far as the eyes can see;
The plain turns yellow with blind skeletons.

Autumn's skirts, carried by the wind,
Transforms themselves in throngs with sharp claws;
Cancerous tumors penetrate nearby homes.
Power! How insignificant Power is!
Hollow stalks are bent by strong gales;
Running time disappears.

Your Hand, Lord, forcefully slaps
The glass and iron face;
Watering eyes hide deep into caverns,
The Antichrist takes the likeness of Your Son,
Sleepwalkers swarm in eagles' bellies;
China shells greedily confine
Empty darkness
Within clenched jaws.

The diseases start with dumbfounded fibers;
Screaming flesh peels off the bones.
Pain gnaws at the house's foundation;
The vulgar, brutal force
Is clearly understood by all.

THE WAVE RETURNS ...

The wave returns,
Washes my feet,
With its soft hand,
Foamy, singing.

"What did you bring me?" I ask
 And up and down I eye
Its offerings of seaweed and salt.

This day will be biting
And way too barren,
The sky is showing its wintry face.
Heavy clouds and a crumpled fragment of the sun
Chase each other.

Moaning, the wave sighs and retreats
Leaving behind ransacked, dirty sand;
Sprays of large salty drops
Hang on stony breakwaters.

A lion-fish howls
Far off in the depths;
A nacreous shard from a stone
Pried from submarine volcanoes,
Throbs at the shores.

The Burden of Defeated Flesh

O, how many tears
Bears the tree
Under the dirty vault!
O, how many tears
Does a man gather
From the scatterbrained thoughts
Of one night!

Permeated to the bones
By vast, unreal euphorias
Fleshy flowers burst out in a vase;
Spreading their heady perfume
With arms of ruffled lace
Greedy courtesans, lazily fondling us.

The exuberance of the tropics
Shamelessly twists;
In a bold, sensuous dance,
Painted flighty skirts
Lustfully caress our faces.

I hear in the distance the venomous rustle
Of great reptiles lagging behind.
They menace and solemnly promise us
The sweetness of death, the slow smothering,
The bitter, profound bite,
Their humble, clammy embrace.

From picture frames, glassy eyes stare at us.
We let ourselves be fascinated
By a few written sheets of paper.
Raspy, drawling voices
Stir us to innermost depths,
The poison of forbidden words
Fills our ears
And we want more.
Into pits oozing of decaying corpses
Foredoomed we slide,
We fall,
Probing, through the entangled moaning,
For the burden of defeated flesh.

In the brothel-like light of the moon
Sleek yellow bellies glow.

EVERYDAY EFFORT

We cling to everyday efforts,
To the blue torment of each night,
We fear that through habit we lose
The sharp pain that makes us proud,
And which, giving a meaning to our existence,
Justifies the signs piously gathered
On our soft faces, in dark rings under our eyes;
Crippled and lofty trees
Sigh under serpents of snow,
We sink under forcible burdens,
All of us, together.

The ship glides along the horizon
Like a worm on the birch bark.
Ash colored fish disappear in the depths,
The lake ices over in a thick blanket.

The shellfish-like day fastens in its tender cores
The pearl-like tears,
A pallid scraping from the starry soul;
The moon's round face,
Hungry, gulps down the absent time,
The longing consumes us again.

Ample terrors, big contradictions,
Weigh on us at length,
The heart comes unhinged from its groove,
We can't feel with our flesh, with our being any more,
The whole world lowers itself
Onto our very grace.

AUTUMN MORNING

This autumn morning
Smiles with steely teeth,
The sea, a calm pond, wakens,
The skin itches, the temple throbs,
Fish teem in mysterious drawers,
Bodies unfurl
      into light.

Yellow clouds spread
Their svelte roots in the sky,
The soul, locked unto itself,
Glides serenely over the desire of the flesh,
Funny names of bearded clowns
Cling to burnt lips.

The night's gestures return furtively
Under harsh glances of children-judges,
Assuaged whispers linger in ether,
The memory endures, rebels,
Spider wings voluptuously descend
Into the sea, an all encompassing tale.

DENSE FOG

The ashen day, crumbled onto itself,
Drips its sweat
On lovers' shoulders.

Dampness penetrates through clothes;
The amorphous fog swallows
A whole continent
With no let up.

Icy fingers tickle us,
The skin shudders;
Important people
And oppressed ones,
Moan bowed over
By a heavy load.

Breath,—a silvery thread—
Wheezes with millions of voices
Air no longer reaching the lungs,
Dissolves into fog
And screams.

MY MOTHER

My mother did not play the piano;
She couldn't find a purpose for
My growing fingers, outstretched,
She wouldn't guide them;
She was unaware
Of the lofty sense of flying,
She had no daring.

My mother did not read
Scholarly books or great literature;
Poetry made her by turns
Laugh or cry;
She would sit quietly humming
Melancholy songs about Jesus,
While the fold on her brow
Obstinately deepened
And her face became
More and more pallid.

My mother didn't know much
About the affairs of this world,
But her smile, like a lamp's flame,
Knew all about everything,
Before fading away, much too soon,
Leaving us holding
All the boundless and hungry darkness
In our arms.

My grandmother knew even less,
But her hands, those sorceresses,
Alternately plaited and unbraided our lives,
Like a transparent kerchief,
A magic word,
A flowering dream
Stretching over the world,
Like a light, gentle breeze.

Thoughtless Hopes

I swept the lady bugs from floors and from walls,
They pretended to be dead.
They were too lazy to run or to fly,
Didn't know spring had arrived.

I had my own plans too:
Expecting prediction from somewhere,
I was softly humming an ancient song,
Thinking all the while what food to pack
For the road.

None of them flies;
They remain here, crouched,
Retreating into the warmth of the room,
Wishing in their turn
For these thoughtless hopes
To cease.

Time on My Shoulders

Something irreversible takes place:
The earth becomes imbued
With the time that passes.
It's raining seconds
Finely, without haste;
We hear the small patter,
Plain,
Inexorable
.

—A vast field,
Life, is waiting:
Sunrise is almost forgotten.
The bluish sunset hovers about,
Crouching round the hill.

We have a handful of minutes still left;
People are sowing them
Step by step,
Into furrows.

Right Now I Know…

I know why, at this moment,
The place where my heart is, hurts,
— a weary box—
I hunger for a world without victorious hordes,
Without defeated people, useless triumphs,
A world with no disasters
and no slavery.

I want to see mankind gather around
The darkest of the rocks,
The wickedest of evil,
Striking the dense fog with bare shoulders,
Determined, to prove their great courage,
And Peace, with its crown of pure light,
Driving away, with wisdom,
The tears from heavy clouds.

Unkempt heroes, with ragged coat tails
Rush singing, through the dust of the road,
Clumsy big birds with an awkward flutter,
Away from the sky
And far from great rewards,
They stumble and then fall, bewildered,
To the nameless, far off, hostile ground.

Angels' Feathers

We remove dainty, slim,
Minuscule angels' feathers
From our clothes;
We take them out, launching them into air,
Watching them as they rise up and soar,
Dashing vertically toward the ceiling,
Thinking that
They could reach through it with no problems,
Toward the void where,
Like withered branches,
The Arms of The Father are waiting.
Tired of us people,
The feathers long to settle
On His sleeves,
Thus becoming again full angels
And come back in the evening
At bedtime,
To guard our sleep
Against the Evil One.

THE PAPER

Pen in hand,
I sit at the table again,
Scribbling across the paper, aimlessly.
Out of wandering thoughts
Rushing into the room
Together with the bees
—Dizzy with the crisp shudder of morning—
Your name appears,
Dancing amid words,
Like a beautiful alabaster God.

Fiery letters pull me into their whirl.
And I don't recall when
Suddenly
 I lost my whole body.
I remain just a voice, whispering to you,
Just a hand, transparently drawing
The miraculous outline of your eyes,
Your pallid brow,
Casting spells, imploring,
Loving you wildly
With all my yearning banished
To these immaculate,
And blind sheets of paper.

CATS' SLEEP

In their sleep,
Cats moan with human-like voices,
They writhe and weep as if
Carrying the world's sorrows
On their backs.

Wild animals slide into sleep
On bitter, salty stairs;
A small bird lies dead under the window
For three days now,
And it rains a sunny rain.

No one grieves, nobody cares
That the lives of others end before their time;
Only through orchards with pockmarked faces
Do bloody tears hang on branches;
Exhaling, ill forests catch fire;
The wind roars and sighs.

Eyes filled with light,
Eyes overtaken by fate,
Trail us everywhere, all the time,
With an endless question mark blossoming,
In their ardent ray.

The Sighing

O, bird as red
As the sun at twilight;
An orange lingering
On the leafless branch.

Through the windows you peer,
A shy messenger;
But who sent you here?
What blizzards?
What turmoil?

Or maybe it was a sigh
That summoned you home,
A frenzied grief
                    making its way through walls,
Maybe it was the flesh,
                    a stretched linen,
A footpath for the pain,
Or the music, the smooth breeze,
Monotonously babbling
Through the veils of the soul.

The bodiless hand strikes at the gate;
Dreamingly, the snarl hovers over us;
Emptied of life,
—At random—
The mantle is drifting.

THREE EAGLES AND THE SPRING

Three eagles
Turn circles,
        hover over chasms;
It's mating time it seems;
Old fir-trees straighten their backs;
Saps chase each other on nest tops.

Somewhere near a young girl cries,
Life is not always
As we'd like it.
Ash colored bees
Lounge in the sun,
A green-eyed maple tree
Sways and tosses about.
The gate stands open halfway.

Wings of large bridges
Vibrating, take me in;
God rests in humid altars;
The shadows of evening
Descend, one by one.

A stony sleep lectures me, goads me
To cut off without mercy
The wing that I urged, no so long ago,
To fly high.
To stop the unpaired, solitary wing,
From soaring far from home,
A bride to the void.

ABSOLUTION

I toil along
Amid dirty snow banks;
February's sun burns me fully,
Blinds me.

Peace—
Everyone asks me for peace,
As if peace
Belonged to me.

Forgiveness—
Everyone asks me for forgiveness
As if I could
Forgive forever.

I pray, like everybody, for redemption of my sins,
At night, in the darkness, at bedtime,
Sometimes on Sundays
Or on blue, cloudless holidays.

You are confusing churches, my beloved;
The place for nocturnal confessions
Is high, far higher.
If you'll just be a little more patient,
Your turn will come, too,
To vent your grief
And repent.
To utter
Whatever else there is to be said.

LEAVES-PETALS

Pink leaves, rendered into petals,
Sneak into the house on soles of unripe animals;
It's for the first time when
                          their tiny muzzles,
Sniff the scent of autumn,
It's for the first time when,
                          God,
Beckons to them too.

Still puzzled, they look around
As at a toy that's been broken.
They clean their soft furs
Of dirty, heavy rain-drops,
Ready to forget all,
                          and especially to forgive;
With eyes full of sun,
To run as in times past
After butterflies and shadows.

ANGEL DRUNK WITH SORROW

O, Palestine,
O, Holy Land…

Mothers must not know
That when we kill others,
we end our lives too;
Mothers must not see
The eyes, the flesh and blood of their own blood
Lying in dirty heaps, piled on the pavement.

Angel, drunk with sorrow,
Take them and guide them
Far from their precious fruits
Cleaved and soft.

Big fires burn across the street;
In lieu of rain, —a withered fog—
In lieu of un-uttered screams
And heavy weeping,
Of rabid hatred.

You still have a few more kids at home, Mother;
In a filthy handkerchief they gather me up, a hero,
Look at the cemetery bare of leaves:
Alone and un-ripened,
There I lay too.

So come on, Mother,
Drop by from time to time,
Hold me again in your arms, I need you,
If you find some time,
And if they allow you to go,
Come, we'll drink cool water,
By the little stream.

What a Beautiful Day!

What a beautiful day!
People surround me, full of kindness,
Friends cast wet flowers for me on blue seas;
Others, climbing high mountains,
Mountains I wasn't aware of
Until today,
Invite me to join them,
If only in my thoughts.

Thoughts, thoughts,
Sweet dreams.
Wild ducks unsettle the morning stillness
With their large, heavy flutter.
Fidgety deer stomp the ground rhythmically.
Somebody knocks at the heart's gates.
A new love awaits me in every airport,
Replacing an old one
With delicate petals,
Broken off from a star.

BABYLON

A bunch of yellow flowers
Scatter in the wind;
"Morocco", snarl rotten teeth;
A bunch of crimson flowers
Quiver in the rain;
"Sri Lanka", sighs the rounded face;
Under scowling glances
Leafless branches
Stoop and groan.

"This kerchief is torn—I want my money back!"
Dark skinned, furrowed foreheads
Frown and sigh;
Worries, a smoky cloud,
Make their way through time.

Cold drops pierce us to the bones,
Through flimsy, summery clothing;
Tears soak ancient skeletons,
The mind is distracted,
The sobbing, deep,
Short-sleeved blouses
Flutter in the wind,
The face slowly withdraws
Into the ground.

AN ANGEL WITHOUT WINGS

On the window ledge an angel stopped,
Confused and trembling,
                  wingless;
His suppliant eyes filled with tears,
Fogged up by many sorrows,
By his turbulent and secret thoughts.

Outside, under the snow, chestnut trees whither;
Just a few days remain until Christmas,
Blue with cold, the footsteps turn numb;
Inside houses, lofty pines glimmer,
Carols herald a fulfilled harvest,
And in this tinseled night
A wingless angel begs at the windows.

And what I am to do? Shall I unlock the bolt?
Shall I let the sweet curse warm itself by the fire?
But then, how will the promised Infant,
born from a star,
Descend into my manger
When the angel destined to serve Him,
Humbled and wingless, with eyes of ink,
Stays crouched under ancient sins,
Carefully hatched year after year,
Dream after dream,
Mistake by mistake.

How Would It Be...

How would it be if I suddenly changed
Into a stately tree in a plain,
Wanting to clasp the heavy passing clouds
To my bosom
Struggling, but unable,
To tear my roots
Out of the deep earth.

How would it be
If the wind put its arms around me,
Enticing me with soft, belated whispers,
Inviting me into its enchanted world,
And I
Much as I'd want to follow it,
Would never, ever dare.

And how would it be
If life came and then left,
Scattering its silvery fragrances
Through my hair,
And I,
Chained to my blessed canons,
Were to shed, one by one,
My many withered leaves,
Which the wind doesn't want,
The cloud doesn't know of,
And that people sweep up, at random.

THE ROOF

Looking out the window I see
Four men covering the neighbor's house.
I spy on their large, calloused hands
And I'm seized by longing,
By joy.

The world has a clear purpose, of course,
We build, we create,
We warm those rough and bony hands
With our white and burning
Breath.

My room delights in young thoughts;
Sure of themselves,
My dreams proceed
Towards their rightful homes.
People help each other, understand;
Nails thrust deeply into layers
Of new asphalt. Covering the nest,
Brightening it,
Making it whole.

WHEN I LEAVE...

When I leave the house, my plants
Writhe panic-stricken.
I hear them rustling behind large curtains,
Whispering anxiously, wondering;
Dear, dear plants,
Their dreamy, fleshy leaves,
Their cheerful fragrant flowers,
Sprinkled with the sun's scintillating beads.

When I leave the house,
So many eyes are left orphaned at the windows;
Dog's eyes, tree's eyes,
The green eyes of a cat, a flower's eyes,
And the urge seizes me sometimes
To retrace my steps and stay
Here, forever enwrapped
In unfulfilled dreams of departures.

It's like that when we love:
We become attached and we suffer;
The moment of good-byes tastes of bitter ash;
Hearts bleed, stabbed by flashy daggers;
Gates close behind us
With infinite unease.

The House Built from a Dance

In the pit adorned with hanging cardboard bats,
Golden fish and real flamingos,
I built myself a house from a dance;
Its paper walls kept growing
In clatter of swing, Latino and samba;

I wandered followed by your smiling eyes,
Amid gray plaster-rocks,
Cold beads of sweat trickled down my back,
With my fingertips I scattered
The water of small pools—
And fish, floating on the surface,
Trailed me.

The house I thought demolished long ago,
Stood now in front of me, out of cardboard;
But the wine became whiter with the passing hours,
Your voice more and more plastered,
And the house built from a dance
Awaited dejected, in rhythms of tangos,
For the harsh breath of a devastating wind,
To knock it down noisily
As happened in other times
As it so often did.

FLYING ANTS

Flying ants land on bare arms, sting,
Crickets and grasshoppers
Hastily call each other
On telephone lines.
The sun descends in a worldly buzz;
Garden tools play hide and seek in tall grasses,
Flowers and omens bow in reverence.

In a melancholy sky,
—In broad daylight—
The moon advances slowly,
Mumbling to itself.

In Packs

When, in packs, we sense
The smell of blood,
We kill each other more easily.
The butcher chooses his victim with care,
The knife plunges into soft necks,
Helpless wings writhe for an instant
Under boots soles.
Death glides calmly over our ankles,
Like a cat's caress,
Like ancient wine trickling through fingers,
Like a question mark, lingering,
In a child's eyes.

Outside, in the morning breeze,
Men with bulging chests ram the ground.
The frightened buck stomps in the mud,
Bustles and shivers feeling the end in its bones,
Its antlers pierce the air for the last time,
Blindly searching for the hidden meaning
Of the great hunt.

ROAD OF AUTUMN

The road, aflame under the soft sun,
Splits the forest in two:
On your side is autumn,
The trees already purple,
Pyres rise proudly,
An incandescent dew.

On my side the foliage is both green and shady,
Young and enticing, under a grain of light,
And my step hurrying toward you,
Jumps and leaps backward through time,
Warmth fills me gaily;
It is utterly summer.

The yellow step,
Both ripe and golden,
And the lithe step,
Jaunty and fast,
Match each other in a colorful dance
Whirling in heaps on sidewalks
Both the green, ancient-copper leaves,
And the blunt, crimson-golden ones.

SOMETHING IS MISSING

Spirits with rainy eyes
Whirl at the windows;
Autumn gathers in its colored palms
The song of the afternoon.

Something is missing:
Tiny birds, holding counsel in the garden,
      align themselves on branches,
Lazy squirrels jump from twig to twig,
The wind breathes gently, playing
Through golden locks.

Something is missing:
A soft, immense void
Weighs down on me.
Stark naked, the sun,
Laughing invades the room;
-I fooled you, he says, the other day,
When I hid into the forest's howling,
Letting the wet snowfall strike your face.
I am back with you today;
Aren't you happy?

I can't be, I'm missing something;
I miss the black little paw, the velvety muzzle,

That something that time
Doesn't dare take away
      and transform,
Into a vague, universal love
For all that lives.

I miss the amber of those profound eyes,
The funny crumb of moon, hidden in pockets,
That something I call for, over and over,
In nights haunted by ghosts,
When fluid shadows change into black cats
Their hair standing on their backs.

That something, wrenched from the depth of my heart,
The feeble equilibrium, dissolved suddenly,
Seized by a gust of wind,
And leaving me waiting,
                              arms outstretched,
While now and then flinging in my path,
A soft bird dropped from the skies
In front of stately, locked gates.

The Day When I Don't Write Poetry

The days when I don't write poetry,
I play hide-and seek with the sun.
Merrily, he slips through paper clouds,
I rise on tiptoes,
Lie in wait,
And when I, bored, give up and leave,
He blinds me laughing.

When I close my eyes,
I see his golden legs under my eyelids.
Glowing fire-swords cut the skyline in strips.
The clock strikes the hour without haste,
The days drag on,
Light retreats under rust colored blankets.

Softly, a mysterious children's game
Slides on the thread of my thought.

Somewhere in the shade
God smiles.

WHEN SOMEONE DIES UNEXPECTEDLY

When someone dies unexpectedly,
Unfinished things lag behind,
Ideas or projects,
Half alive and
Half spent.

Mother had prepared dishes for her children,
To last them a whole week.
Mother's hands of pure gold,
A tender, ardent, memory
Lingering around for days to come,
Setting the table,
Washing the dishes,
Gently serving food into plates.

Once Upon a Time...

Once upon a time
I tasted doves' meat.
I indulged in
Legs of rabbits and lambs;
I have eaten also from the flesh of meek horses,
Sacrificed in their turn,
On hunger's altar.

I took in the Eucharist from all that lived.

Verily I say unto you:
The pigeon or rabbit steak
Is extraordinarily tasty:
It smells like grass, like broken earth
                              in the spring,
Like a writhing wing
Carried off by the wind
In the evening.

About horses' meat,
About the bitter taste,
Of bleeding,
Large hearts,
I do not remember,
I no longer know.

CASTAWAYS

At last, I ran aground on shore,
A shore strewn with broken glass,
Where hopeless ships lean stranded
On their sides.

From their hulky bodies abandoned in the sand,
From their rusted, cracked bellies,
Large patches of oil
Spread over the ocean
Into the distance.

The wave returns, flinging onto the beach
More bodies discarded by the waters:
Under midday's merciless sun,
Small birds with ember eyes
Leaven, silted in death.

From the sand I pick up a bottle,
A note, tossed at random
A long time ago,
The message, misted over
by shells and algae,
Was surely once a cry for help,
A humble voice
That no longer expects any answer,
And that is sleeping now
In a light sleep.

I rock the alien sorrow in my arms,
As I would rock my own;
This wandering sob,
That started in some far off place,
Becomes one with mine at this shore,
Finding a long wished-for peace
In an undulating
Burial whisper.

Immortality

Every day they bring
A new corpse into the church;
All my friends are also ill;
Gasping for air, the city toils under dust;
Its streets teem with stray dogs,
From deep in the shade
A cat, meowing, begs.
Pavements clasp the day's torridness
To a stony bosom.

Confused,
The thought stops in flight,
Biding time.

THE END OF THE WORLD

It seems that the end of the world is nearing
When tens of thousands of birds
Suddenly fall from the sky,
The silky burden covers the plains
Like a downy carpet,
A funereal jewel.

Armies of freckled and shaggy insects
Quickly invade young trees,
Driving tunnels through soft barks to the cores,
Hurried mandibles penetrate live flesh;
Exhausted forests wither and die.

People of means copy their own likeness,
Chimeras they build from the dust—
Children of woman unborn,
Lie in white test tubes,
Impatiently, in wait.

December, January, February,
Another year passes in three months;
Alien grief clings to my clothes,
Fear, like a sigh, penetrates all my pores,
Question marks thrust into my forehead
Like a red, thorny wreath.

NOTE

Solitude first appeared in Poetry Salzburg Review Nr. 10, Autumn 2006

Reverie, Road of Autumn, Angels' Feathers, The Omens, At Dawn, Spider-Like Star, Midnight Thoughts, Vapid Love, An Angel Without Wings and *Autumn Morning* first appeared in Comparative Critical Studies 5, published by British Comparative Literature Association 2008.

Finding You Again first appeared in Revista Cultural Paralelo 30, Brazil, January 2009

The End of the World first appeared in Private, International Review of Black and White Photographs and texts, Nr. 42, autumn 2008

The Roof first appeared in Our Times, Canada's Independent Labor Magazine, September 2009

A number of poems from *In the Arms of the Father* were included in *Gothic Calligraphy*, a chapbook published by Červená Barva Press, Somerville, MA, 2007

About The Co-Translator

Charles Siedlecki is an educator, writer, translator and poetry editor living and working in Toronto, Canada. He received a degree in English Literature and Art History from the University of Toronto, and later took a fellowship at AKADEMIA SZTUK PIEKNYCH w WARSZAWIE (The Warsaw Academy of Fine Arts).

He received the Third Prize in the 2007 Dryden Translation Competition for co-translating together with Flavia Cosma her poetry book *In the Arms of the Father*—prize awarded by British Comparative Literature Association/British Centre for Literary Translation.

Charles Siedlecki's poetry collection *Somewhere in the Universe* was published by KCLF-21 Press, Toronto in 2008.

About the Author

Flavia Cosma is a Romanian-born Canadian writer, poet and translator. She is also a professional photographer and producer, director and screenwriter for television documentary films.

Flavia has published poetry, prose, children's literature and travel memoirs. Her books were translated and published in various countries and languages. Flavia has a Master's in Electrical Engineering from the Polytechnic Institute of Bucharest, Romania. Cosma's poetry books *Leaves of a Diary, Thus Spoke the Sea* and *The Latin Quarter* were studied at Universities in Canada and USA during the school years 2008, 2014 and 2017. A recipient of several international literary awards Flavia Cosma is the director of The Biannual Writers' and Artists' Festivals at Val-David, Quebec, Canada.

www.flaviacosma.com
flaviacosma9@gmail.com

Selected Publications

English Publications :

Eternal Returning/Eterno Ritorno, poems, bilingual edition English/Italian, 2019, Giuliano Ladolfi Editore, Italy, ISBN 978-88-6644-432-9

The Latin Quarter, poems, 2016, MadHat Press, Asheville, North Carolina, USA, ISBN 978-1-941196-21-2

On Paths Known to No One, poems, 2012, Cervena Barva Pres, Somerville, Massachusetts, USA, ISBN 978-0-9844732-6-7

Postcards from Rhodes, a travel memoir, 2010, Variety Crossing Press, Toronto, Canada, ISBN 978-0-9812279-2-4

Moonlight Fairy Tales, a children's book, 2009, In Our Own Words Inc. Press, Mississauga, ON, Canada, ISBN 978-0-9809932-8-8

Thus Spoke the Sea, poems, 2008, KCLF-21 Press, Toronto, ON, Canada, ISBN 978-0-9782020-6-4. 80 pages.

The Season of Love, poems, 2008, Červená Barva Press, Somerville, MA, USA, ISBN 978-0-615-20097-2, 89 pages.

A Country of One, an E-book, www.brindin.com 2007,100 pages

The Adventures of Tommy Teddy Bear and Alex Little Bunny, a children's book, 2007, Korean-Canadian Literary Forum-21 Press, Toronto, ON, Canada, ISBN 0-9782020-1-9

Gothic Calligraphy, a poetry chapbook, 2007, Červená Barva Press, Somerville, Massachusetts, USA

Leaves of a Diary, poems, 2006, Korean-Canadian Literary Forum-21 Press, Toronto, Canada, ISBN 0-9689561-7-3, 72 pages.

Fata Morgana, poems, 2003, Edwin Mellen Press, Lewiston, NY, ISBN 0-7734-3482-8, 87 pages.

Wormwood Wine, poems, 2004, 2001, Edwin Mellen Press, Lewiston, NY, ISBN 0-7734-3416-X, ISBN 0-7734-3553-0 (hc), 87 pages.

The Fire that Burns Us, a novel, 1996, Singular Speech Press, Canton, Connecticut, ISBN 1-880286-34-3, 114 pages.

47 POEMS, 1992, Texas Tech University Press, ISBN 089672-304-6, ISBN 0-89672-279-1, 99 pages. (Richard Wilburn ALTA Poetry in Translation Award)

Fairy Tales by Flavia Cosma, 1990, Canadian Stage and Arts, Toronto, Canada, ISBN 0-919952-48-8, 47 pages.

FRENCH PUBLICATIONS :

Temps de moisson, poèmes, 2021, Éditions du Cygne, Paris, France, ISBN : 978-2-84924-649-8

Fauves et ombres, poèmes, 2017, Éditions du Cygne, Paris, France,

ISBN 978-2-84924-501-9

Griffures sur le miroir, poèmes, 2015, Éditions du Cygne, Paris, France, ISBN 978-2-84924-423-4

Quartier latin, poèmes, octobre 2014, Éditions du Cygne, Paris, France, ISBN 978-2-84924-378-7, 75 pages

Le corps de la lune, poèmes, mai 2014, Éditions du Cygne, Paris, France, ISBN 978-2-84924-359-6, 82 pages

Le miel trouble du matin, poèmes, 2012, L'Harmattan, Paris, France, ISBN 978-2-296-96071-8, 144 pages

Spanish Publications :

Tiempo de cosecha, 2019, Mirada Malva, Granada, España, ISBN 978-84-120205-3-3, 90 paginas

Cuentos de hadas a la luz de la luna, 2018, Mirada Malva, Granada, España, ISBN 978-84-948523-0-5, 60 paginas

Fieras y sombras, poemas, 2018, Mirada Malva, Granada, España, ISBN 978-84-945681-8-3, 79 paginas

Arañazos sobre la faz del espejo, poemas, 2015, Ediciones Torremozas, Madrid, España, ISBN 978-84-7839-618-4

El cuerpo de la luna, poemas 2013, Editorial Maribelina, Lima, Perú, ISBN 978-9972-685-46-0, 73 paginas

El barrio latino, poemas 2012, Editorial Maribelina, Lima, Peru, ISBN 978-9972-685-42-2, 90 paginas

Hojas de diario, poemas 2011, Editorial Maribelina, Lima, Peru

Plumas de ángeles, poemas, 2008, Editorial Dunken, Buenos Aires, Argentina, ISBN 978-978-02-3508-8, 87 paginas

Romanian Publications :

Vremea culesului, poeme, Editura Ars Longa 2018, Iasi Romania, ISBN

Cine ne sunt îngerii, proza poetica, EditurA Ars Longa 2017, Iasi, Romania

Sălbăticiuni şi umbre, poeme, ISBN 978-973-148-212-5, Editura Ars Longa, 2015, Iasi, Romania

Linişte divină, poeme, ediţie bilingvă româno/albaneză, ISBN 978-9951-02-232-8, Editura Amanda Edit Verlag, 2015, Bucureşti, România, 120 pagini

Zgârieturi pe faţa oglinzii, poeme, ISBN 978-973-148-150-0, Editura Ars Longa, 2013, Iasi, Romania

Trupul lunii, poeme, ISBN 978-973-148-111-1, Editura Ars Longa, 2012, Iasi, Romania, 101 pages

Pe căi de nimeni ştiute, poeme, ISBN 978-973-148-074-9, Editura Ars Longa, 2011, Iasi, Romania, 102 pages

Focul ce ne arde, roman, ISBN 978-973-148-075-6, Editura Ars Longa, 2011, Iasi, Romania, 180 pages

Cartierul latin, poeme, ISBN 978-973-148-073-2, Editura Ars Longa, 2011, Iasi, Romania, 87 pages

Poveşti sub clar de lună/ Contes de fées,(ediţie bilingvă

Română/Franceză), Editura Ars Longa, 2009, Iaşi Romania, ISBN 978-973-148-028-2, 151 pages

*Neant binevoitor,*poeme, Semne Press, 2007, Bucharest, Romania, ISBN 978-973-624-533-6, 103 pages

Cântece la marea Egee, poeme, Editura Ars Longa, 2007, Iaşi, Romania, ISBN 978-973-8912-74-8, 71 pages

Teatru pentru copii mici şi mari, EdituraFamilia 2007, Oradea, Romania, ISBN 978-973-9401-73-9, 58 pages

In braţele Tatălui, poeme, 2006, Editura Cogito, Oradea România, ISBN 973-8032-52-0, 88 pages.

Rhodos sau Rhodes sau Rodi, Jurnal Sentimental, Oct. 2005, Editura Limes, Cluj, România, ISBN 973-726-093-7, 150 pages

Jurnal, poeme, 2004, Editura Cogito, Oradea, România, ISBN 973-8032-35-0, 68 pages

Amar de primăvară, poeme, 2003, Editura România Liberă, Bucharest, România, ISBN 973-86308-8-6, 83 pages

Cină cu demoni, poeme, 1999, Editura Eminescu, Bucharest, România, ISBN 973-22-0759-0, 91 pages

Păsări și vise, poeme, 1997, Editura Eminescu, Bucharest, România, ISBN 973-22-0589-X, 84 pages